Notes
From
My
Phone*

NOTES FROM MY PHONE* Copyright © 2016, text by Michelle Junot. All rights reserved, except for brief quotations in critical articles or reviews. No part of this book may be reproduced in any manner without prior written permission from the publisher, Mason Jar Press.

Design and layout by Ian Anderson.

First U.S. Edition: September 2016

Published and distributed by Mason Jar Press
Baltimore, MD 21218

Learn more about Mason Jar Press at masonjarpress.xyz.

Notes From My Phone*

*A self-portrait in her twenties.

Michelle Junot

9:59 AM
The notes section of my phone may be my most-telling memoir.

November 23, 2014

A Note on Notes

This collection was written by accident and in pieces. It was never intended to be a book, only lists or wonderings or desperate prayers written down to help me get through a hectic day. Most days. For five years. Instead, the notes took on a life of their own, forming an unintended time capsule of who I was, who I was becoming, and who I am now.

I was on a plane speeding down a runway on the outskirts of Baltimore when I found it. I wasn't sure what to do with it, but verbs like "delete" or "burn" came to mind. I told a few friends about it and "tested it" on my blog. There wasn't much response except from one friend who said "Don't get rid of it. Hold on to it. Seriously. Do something with it."

So I continued to take notes—somewhat self-consciously—if only to remember to get contact solution at the store.

Two years later, that friend asked to publish it, and here we are. This is the last piece of the last draft—the only section of the collection I've intentionally set out to write—and I'm still feeling uncertain about the whole project. But I think that's okay.

If there's one thing I've learned from this self-portrait in her twenties, it's that life isn't about us knowing how all our decisions will play out. Life is often about not knowing and taking the step anyway. It's about taking risks sometimes—putting yourself out there, knowing it's going to be uncomfortable. Knowing you might fail. And ultimately, it all comes back to knowing that at the end of the day, even if your life is completely messed up (and even if you're the reason it's completely messed up), you're okay.

You're already loved and cared for and seen and known, even in your complete messiness.

So without further stalling, here it is—albeit ripped from my knuckled, closed-fist grip.

For all the women who taught me strength through their vulnerability.

〉slide to unlock

9:37 AM
We often picture an outcome and work backwards from that vision, but creativity is about working forward, not necessarily having a concept of where you're going.

⟨ Michelle's Notes

2:44 PM
at the airport
    stereotypical rich family:
    father and son in khakis and matching navy sports coats, cheeks flushed
    daughters in tight jeans and leather boots to their knees
        or daughter, singular, and mother (it's hard to tell)

grown men with tiny backpacks holding the hands of their small children
    or what I hope are *their* children
looking around for the arrivals and departures while answering children's questions

children walking where their hands are led,
but looking around with wide eyes at all the people

an angry-looking woman holding a large bag with the word LOVE printed on its side

girls wearing boots
other girls wearing boots with calf-expanders

little girls pulling suitcases that are pink with Minnie Mouse's face on them
another featuring Barbie
    one also carries a stuffed rabbit, only by the ear

babies in strollers that are tagged with the same tags as my luggage

two small girls waving bye to each other as their families and hands are led in opposite directions,
like tiny adults setting out on their own journeys

> and it's unclear if they knew one another before crossing paths in the airport
> or if they're strangers
> because the parents do not wave or say goodbye and one actually scolds his child for screaming across the airport,
> embarrassed by her dramatic outburst

other parents following stumbling toddlers, picking up stumbling toddlers, and bringing screaming toddlers back to the starting point when they've ventured too far.

> toddlers crying because they didn't know they were being followed

a father asking, "do you want to hold your own ticket?"

> a father immediately regretting his offer as grabby kids reach for the thin paper

Michelle's Notes

> "never mind," he says, tucking them all back into his pocket
> an announcement: pre-boarding
>> military, dressed in uniform,
>> along with those with special needs and families with children
>> line of able-looking bodies form ahead of the soldiers

promoted to first class — Facebook status updated

> receive more likes on first-class status than my acceptance to grad school status
> not that Facebook is a true measure of our society and its values

> oh wait. yes it is.

I want to write about language in first class, but the language isn't different
it's the props that are changed

> for example, they still ask, "would you like something to drink?"
> and I still say, "Coke"

but it comes in a real glass—like a drinking instrument made from glass

and my eyes are larger, my cheeks redder when I say thank you

adult beverages?

< Michelle's Notes

10:11 PM
Baggage claim: why does everyone wait in exactly the same spot?

3:54 PM
Things to do with Favorite:

    fried rice and pad thai
    bookstore by the baby Wal-Mart

    go hiking and backpacking
        but we have to go in a place with no bears

< Michelle's Notes

7:43 AM
contact solution
oil

office depot
groceries

      milk
      berries
      corn
      meat

9:22 AM

Sometimes, I can't sleep because I'm wondering why you ended things the way you did—one day saying you loved me and the next that you just couldn't do it anymore.

> What about the good stuff?
>
>> The laughing. The inside jokes. The merh and the jaaaas.
>> The things that were *so us* that I can't even remember when they started or where they came from.

What about the nook I fit into when I curled up beside you? Or all the new games long distance afforded us? What happened to being my best friend?

What about dancing?

> You thought it best to wait until our hypothetical union, and I was more interested in dancing alone together in a room at your apartment. But you could never open yourself up even to that small thing.

So maybe I should have known then that you never planned to dance with me. Our hypothetical marriage

Michelle's Notes

and our hypothetical dates in Baltimore and our hypothetical love were all musings for you.

For me, they were delayed but probable possibilities.

Is that why you ended things? You didn't want to play pretend anymore? Did you realize that my expectations of you and your commitment was becoming real? Why didn't you know that a year ago? Why did you come back with promises?

But more than all that, why did I believe you?

I chose you. I chose to stand up for you to friends and family who understood our problems before I did. I thought I loved you.

But now,

I hate you for it.

6:16 AM

I turned over, and grabbed my too dark and too cold phone. You hadn't called. I was dreaming.

You weren't missing me. You were probably sleeping just as soundly as you always did, 1,000 miles away. And that realization was the most painful yet.

That's when I realized that I'd scratched my elbow raw in my sleep; I was bleeding.

< Michelle's Notes

8:20 AM
Fat   22%
Waist   27.75
Hips   34.5
Waist   32.5
Thigh   21
Arms   10
Bust   35
Calf   12.75
Knee   13

11:57 PM
My heart is breaking,
and you're the only one I feel like I can talk to.

Mostly because you're hypothetical.

       This sucks.

< Michelle's Notes

9:56AM
eggs
milk

4:30 AM

I keep having these nightmares, trapped in dreams with people who don't love me anymore. I didn't even try leaving that last one when I've always known how.

Instead, my subconscious dragged me out by my arms and my equilibrium, and I woke up with the ringing of my own dream-scream in my ears, paralyzed awake. And the last thing I saw was their world right itself, like I was in *Alice in Wonderland* and they'd just realized I didn't belong.

So he'll be fine, going on in the upside down world where he doesn't love me and he doesn't miss me, and doesn't remember how effortlessly "in love" we were. And happy we were. And grounded we were. And I'll continue flipping over scenery, waking up and wondering if we were always in a dream and I only just recently started waking up.

But mostly, I wonder about you.

What do you look like? What do you think about my dreams and my nightmares and my letters? Are you just a resolved me? A lonely me? Or are you a you that understands all these things in addition to yourself? Where are you right now, and how many worlds do I have to turn over to find you and your arms and our safe, dreamless bed?

< Michelle's Notes

11:12 PM
Why does remembering childhood make people sad?
How come we long for what's been instead of marveling at what is?

3:15 PM
music pulling me out
trying to work through my restlessness
need to move
can't choreograph, but I can drive
making my way through another place
making the outside fit inside
working through it is like working through a labyrinth
getting lost is the best way to get found

woke up from another bad dream
blending old and new
trying to figure out where I'm going before I ever really know where I'm from

Baltimore is mine

thought people were the same at heart, but this isn't true
it's naïve
people value different things

words have no meaning or
a word's meaning being recreated over and over again
like city

circling around and around something
maybe that's just life
creating or waiting for things to happen

< Michelle's Notes

9:30 PM
They don't have a blog? Do they?
Probably. Who cares?

9:07 PM
the stadium is new
and so are the stoplights
the Sonic is gone
there's the movie theater from my almost-first-kiss

the back way to school
turning the corner to the most beautiful sunrise

now, Mickey's face looks back at me
from posters on every pole

I've been worrying about running into people I know,
but I don't know these people anymore

⟨ Michelle's Notes

11:02 PM
There are just some things you can't capture with a picture or a memory.

You have to appreciate them fully in their moment, knowing they're only for you and that you'll never be able to fully describe it exactly as it happened to someone else.

9:16 PM
at the walk-in clinic:

    un-decorating the Christmas Tree
    it's November; that seems premature (or incredibly late)

Name?
Birthdate?
Where do you work?
Phone number?
    Home
    Work
    Cell
Emergency contact?
    Should that be my boyfriend?
    No, it's my mom.
Marital status?
Where do you live?
    Seemed to know it was Maryland, but wasn't sure how it was spelled

    HGTV in the background

What brings you here?
What do you do?

< Michelle's Notes

      Better tinsel on the tree now
      Redecorating has begun

The scale
    Oh no. Not the scale.
Yeah, the scale.

Blood pressure
    Just relax

    Martha and I joking about her being my girlfriend

X-rays
    So it's your right hand?
    No, it's my left.
    Wait, it's your left hand?
    Yes, my left.
    You're right, left.

6:41 PM
At the coffee shop, two little boys waiting just inside the door with their mother:
"Why is daddy always the one that has to get the umbrella?"

< Michelle's Notes

7:28 PM
I need to write. There's an itch in my fingers, but the words aren't in my head.

There are seasons when all I can do is revise, but I cannot create anything new. In other seasons, I cannot revise at all. Instead I want to bury everything I've ever written. Start over. Become a different writer—a better writer.

And then there's this season: I'm deep in thought most of the time, and when I'm not, I'm in conversation with people I trust—mining for memory and understanding. For feeling and a sense of purpose in their lives or mine.

> I call this my *almost* season or on the cusp of something season. (I'm not saying it's a good name, that's just what I call it.)

It's hard to know where I go from here when I've suddenly remembered words like *purpose* and *calling* and *faith*.

> How do I write anything worthy of being read when I'm so aware of all the ways I am lacking?

Joshua would tell me to pray, because, for Joshua, the answer is *always* prayer. That's always his answer. But maybe that's because it always is the answer.

< Michelle's Notes

4:56 PM
Bobby pins
Pine cones
Toilet paper

3:21 PM
Grocery Store

There's a man yelling at the milk
little girls cutting me off

another man yelling about
how he might be sick this weekend
    talking on the phone about a very personal thing

woman slaps her child and my eyes tear

I take on the self-check out
    where machines announce everything I'm buying
        and the associated costs

< Michelle's Notes

2:44 PM
3 minutes Row machine
Low intensity

5 minutes Elliptical
Level 1—forward and backward
Medium intensity

Adductor machine
15 @ 40 lbs. bottom rung
Medium intensity

Abductor machine
15 @ 40 lbs. bottom rung
Medium intensity

Low Row machine
20 @ 30 lbs. each side
Low intensity—add more weight

Vertical Traction machine
20 @ 20 lbs.
Medium intensity—could add a little more weight

Leg Curl machine
15 @ 20 lbs. (rigged)
Medium intensity

Leg Extension
15 @ 20 lbs. (rigged)
Medium intensity

Leg Press machine
15 @ 80 lbs.
Medium/High intensity

24% body fat

⟨ Michelle's Notes

4:43 PM
Post Office

Woman wearing sunglasses—indoors—and tights covered in palm trees with a heavy-looking brown coat with fur trim

People in front of me talking algorithms, and someone else wearing an Amelia Earhart hat

1, 2, 3, 15 people in line

The woman behind the desk shouts: "Anyone just dropping stuff off?"

> those who nod yes are directed to the front

> I wish they'd scream, "Anyone budgeted their time poorly?"

Person after person who clearly hasn't rehearsed his speech and request (as I have) make it to the front of the desk:

Stamps. Tax refunds. Confusion.

Other people move against the flow of traffic

"See you at school!" and
"There's a Raven's shirt for my five-year-old nephew in here. Are you a fan?"

The woman behind the desk does not look like she's a fan of much.

My turn.

< Michelle's Notes

3:55 AM
I just had a dream, and I can't help but feel it proves something about my usefulness should this situation ever really come up:

> It was the zombie apocalypse, or the start of it at least—dead monkeys in banana trees (although we still ate the bananas, which is worrisome). I was sent for supplies.
>
> These are some of the things I got:
>
>> Clif bars,
>> the rest of the fresh fruit,
>> the lasagna I happened to be making,
>> my laptop and journal,
>> Clif bars,
>> more bananas,
>> some blankets,
>> more socks,
>> a bunch of decks of cards and three die (one just had printed numbers),
>> a hammer and a wrench,
>> a few old coats and blankets,
>> a knife (but if I'm being honest, I wasn't going to tell anyone I had it),

and the document that Rachel had just brought back from the lab on why all the monkeys were dead,

though she'd just gotten vertigo and I was about to leave the house without her.

⟨ Michelle's Notes

3:00 PM
Learning about Jesus is like learning ballet as a small child. There comes a time when what you've come to know as real has to be broken or challenged by something greater in order to understand the truth.

And that can be a painful process.

10:53 PM
One day, Lord, the days I await will be here and I will be sad because time has moved so quickly.

I will long for time to move in its slow meandering way, the way it feels tonight when everything is so uncertain. My love for you is certain, Lord, although I confess it hasn't always been so.

Lord, I've spent a long evening in the company of a wonderful friend who was able to listen and love me in a way I haven't been loved before. I was heard, and I feel grateful for that.

And yet, I missed him. I'd talked so much about him — the qualities I admired, the struggles we'd faced, and the uncertainty of our future. Lord, I love him and yet my heart believes you are steering me a different way. You may have us on different courses from one another.

I'm afraid.

What have I done? Why have I opened up my heart to this man who doesn't seem to want me in that way? Help me to guard my heart daily. To avoid thoughts of him, desires for him. Let me fully rest in you who desires me more than anyone else.

< Michelle's Notes

Let me seek your comfort, for I know that you desperately want a relationship with me, and will pursue me to the ends of the earth. You are true love, Lord, and I'm joyful to be here with you tonight.

3:04 PM
Girl using beer can to ice her swollen cheek.

< Michelle's Notes

12:09 AM
Speak French
Learn to play piano
Dance again
Read and read a lot
Become really smart
Read the entire Bible
Know God's plan for my heart
Paint a lot
Know how truly blessed I am
Finish my scrapbooks once and for all
Stop collecting crap
Stop seeking a man
Just be thankful
Sleep

I just want to sleep, Lord
Grant me that, please

10:12 AM
My number still hasn't been called.

< Michelle's Notes

11:58 PM
What I really want to know is how I end up—what's the end of the story?

But here's the thing:

> Maybe I don't actually want to know.
> Maybe none of us really want to know.
> Because if I'd known I'd fall in love with a man or two or three who didn't or couldn't or thought he shouldn't love me back, I might have never tried at all.
>
> And then where would I be?

Growing up is critical. Knowing how it will end should be avoided. Because hope is what we run on, and without hope, we'd all be lost.

1:04 PM
God, I need help.

⟨ Michelle's Notes

2:35 PM
Two more shelves with slightly longer brackets

2:57 AM

Lord, I'm tired, and I'm awake again. I'm exhausted from insomnia at night, and I'm never fully awake during the day. I want to take comfort in you, rest in the fact that you have a plan for me. Rest in your grace and deep love for me. Rest in the fact that those feelings and desires and misunderstood heartache will go away soon.

But how will it go away if I don't let go of it?

I feel myself clinging to it, fists wrapped tight around something I thought you'd given me to protect. To guard and trust. What's the point of trusting, Lord? Or working at that—at really breaking down walls—if it's now all crashed down around my feet?

What lesson about love should I draw from that? How do I understand you in that shattered place? Am I broken only to know I need you? Is that what this is about?

I want to understand. I want to follow and trust and love you in all things. I want this rejection to be removed from my memory. I want the pain to stop rising up in my throat when I try to breathe.

The days are fine—I'm busy with tasks, and my heart forgets that it's broken. My heart forgets that it's not

Michelle's Notes

wanted by the one I want. Even saying it now, I see the problem: you cannot be with someone who doesn't want you. And so then there's this battle between my heart and my head—knowing the truth, knowing the Truth, and not feeling the warm comfort of either.

I'm living in this disconnected place where my head wants to praise you for all the good you've done, believing and trusting in the promise you've honored time and time again—first with the Israelites and so often in my own life—but I'm not there. My journals show prayer after broken prayer, many without much thought of you at all. They show me what I couldn't see when I wrote them: hope was around the corner. There would come a time when I wouldn't always feel that way.

My head has seen what you do with time, but my heart's memory is short.

So here I am: awake. Exhausted. I'm fighting everything, including sleep, because the quiet reminds me of all that isn't. My body feels crumpled by the weight of exhaustion and melodramatic tears that come from not sleeping for months. And want. And a deep need to understand.

Lord, I need your real, physical embrace. I need your arms. Your soothing voice. I need you in my humanness. My head and my heart are battling it out, and they're too busy with one another to lull me to sleep.

I'll breathe, Lord. I'll concentrate on that piece because it's the only thing I feel sure I know how to do. Forgive my weakness, but can you do the rest?

> I'll just breathe, and you do all the rest.
> Just for tonight.
> So I can sleep.

‹ **Michelle's Notes**

9:24 PM
I really like figs.
I sleep better when the doors are closed.
Most people think I'm pretty great.
Those who know me know that there are some pretty-not-great things about me,
    but they love me still.

My preference for red wine over white is only getting stronger.

5:46 AM
Arms
Shower
Get ready for work
Breakfast
Ready for class
Bind journal
Go to work
Run this afternoon
Groceries

Michelle's Notes

3:54 AM

John let me borrow this really cute hoodie, but I was supposed to return it to him at the corner of 30th and 36th.

I started running the wrong way, but the person I was with—who was now waiting for me at the 7-Eleven—was being a pain, and I didn't want them to see me run back in that direction, so I took the next block.

But in doing that, I was suddenly at the harbor and I couldn't find a bridge to get across the water. I kept jogging alongside, running parallel, looking for a way to cross, but all of a sudden there were fire hoses aimed at me—some keeping me from getting too close and others closing off my route that pushed me this way in the first place.

I called out to some people that I "wanted to get a picture" and they sent me up to this makeshift bridge that didn't go anywhere.

I ended up in Marion's class and was trying to make an announcement, but she never heard me and kept cutting me off so I left, unheard.

6:25 AM
Strong
Healthy
Hydrated
Rested

< Michelle's Notes

7:32 AM
Eggs
Yogurt
Fruit for yogurt
Pears
Peaches
Milk
Half and half

Ziploc bags
Contact solution

9:45 PM

Clean out my email
Clean the apartment
Finish the rules piece

Pick up dry cleaning
Contact solution
Write a blog
Finish journal
Set up meeting

Work out plan and new goals
Clean the car
Master to-do list
Time for devotional

< Michelle's Notes

8:12 AM
Contact solution
Hand soap

Fruit
Celery
Onion
Veggie dip

Granola
Crackers
Yogurt
Half and half
Mozzarella cheese
Swiss cheese
Colby Jack cheese
Orange juice

Eggs

5:24 PM
Dude. Seriously. You need contact solution.

Michelle's Notes

7:30 AM
I dreamt that he was never in love with me.
He looked at me like I was crazy. He pitied me.

My father was there, showing me how to roll maps, and my father's friend was there, asking why I hadn't bet on horses yet.

10:02 PM
God, I'm avoiding you.

Because facing you means facing the fact that this is part of your plan. That you're okay with my hurting. That you know my heart aches and still we aren't together because we aren't supposed to be. Facing you means letting him go in a real way. It's time. And still the thought makes me nauseous.

Where are you, Lord? And where is your truth in this situation? And where do I go now?

‹ Michelle's Notes

9:59 PM
Heart Memories

> The first time I rode the bus,
> I forgot my backpack
>
> My first school play
>
> Miss Flo taught me how to bowl:
> thinking about holding a bucket of water with my thumb out
> Listening to trains to fall asleep
>
> The first time my car got broken into
> and Adam taking me to get a snowball
>
> Always having a plan when going over a bridge

7:43 AM
Clean up
Clothes
Kitchen
Kitchen counters
Trash
Bathroom
Vacuum
Floors

Make grocery list
Pralines
Pecan pie
Caramel apples
Booze
Water filter
Gumbo
Plastic cups
Bowls
Etc.

Swiffer filters

6:34 PM
Koko

11:18 PM
God, is this really your plan for my life?

Sometimes it seems so uninspired. I don't mean that disrespectfully, I just mean...I don't know what I mean. I just wish I understood what was of you and what wasn't.

I'm attracted to Dillon, but I don't know if I should pursue it. And honestly, I don't know how not to pursue it now that I've mentioned it a few times. Perhaps the distance from him and the city will help out on that front a bit.

God, please give me clarity and direction.
Give me drive and your will and the courage to trust in your plan and provision.

Michelle's Notes

8:17 AM
The roller thing on my hands: yeah, okay.
It's stuff-side down.

> "Have a good day."
> You don't really mean that, do you?

Michelle Rasputin

> "I like Michelle"
> Do I shout out? Hey! That's my name!

She doesn't look pregnant and
the other baby looks way too old not to have a name.

"If you have 'sky' as your zone on your boarding pass, you are welcome to board now."

Oh. They're going to the sky…? Wait. Aren't we all supposed to be doing that?

> Seven strollers and a car seat

10:02 AM
I thought our airport was small, but at least we have sides.

We have at least two sides in ours.

< Michelle's Notes

11:12 PM
God, today was better. Thank you for that.

Please help me to remember that thinking about Joshua is a decision. I can decide to acknowledge that I miss him and his friendship, and then I can move on with my day. I don't need to be consumed with longing for what isn't and what will not be.

Help me to be content with today and all the promises you are fulfilling in my life at this very moment, and give me the courage to realize the ways you may be using me in the lives of others.

Show me the desires of my own heart, and help me to hope for the desires and plans you've set for me. Let me not be troubled or my heart hardened.

11:15 PM
Lord, are you being silent?

I want a relationship with you, Lord, but I also run away from you, and I'm also scared of you at times. I'm scared of your comfort, and I'm scared what following you might actually mean. I still want it to work out despite seeing that it's not working. Lord, I recognize how delusional and stubborn I'm being. I long to let it go. To walk away. And yet, my heart says, "hope."

How can this be? How can I know what is of you and what is my own selfishness? How do I learn to trust and follow you when my own heart gets in the way?

Lord, please pour out your wisdom and understanding on me. Pour it out on me in abundance so that I may love unselfishly and unyieldingly. Make me an instrument of your peace and hope. Help me to think of myself last and to not minimize the cross.

< Michelle's Notes

10:14 AM
It wasn't what I'd expected, but I guess nothing is.

We went there to help people, but also, I went because it meant a stamp in my passport.

2:06 PM
Coffee
Soy sauce

< Michelle's Notes

12:35 AM
I just walked into the apartment
   after a night of drinking and talking with a friend.

The apartment was dark as I walked back to the bedroom. I pretended you were sleeping already, quietly taking off my shoes and my dress. I thought about slipping in beside you. Considered cuddling up to your warmth, kissing your neck and wrapping my arms around you.

And I smiled at it. The possibility of it. The probability of it a year ago—maybe even six months ago.

   Instead, I got in the cold bed, longing for the bar—anywhere else but here.

3:00 AM

It's 3 o'clock in the morning, and I'm still awake. And there's a guy that lives above me who's building a highway or a bowling alley or something of the like. Because he's a maniac.

I have all these pieces of my life to sort through—my ex-boyfriend (did I mention that I dated the landlord?), my family and their expectations, work and all those meetings that make me feel ant-like, and my plants keep dying.

I'm old and smart enough to realize that none of my problems are actually that problematic. I mean, who hasn't dated the landlord? (Well, actually, that one isn't quite as common I'm finding out.) I should say, who hasn't dated the wrong guy? In fact, I'm rather ordinary, but I'm also young. And young people always think that what's happening right now is the absolute worst thing that has ever happened to anyone in the entire world!

Basically, what I'm saying is that I can't even.

< Michelle's Notes

3:03 PM
Birthday party.

    What's in that bottle?

They'll come to my place.
    Can I drive the train?
        Got to be able to drive a bus first.

Oh, there are levels to this shit.

Can't just let anyone from the street operate the train…
    Just jump on the train.
        I paid my ticket.

Because you're white.

8:30 AM
Write about the fridge noise

They left a door tag
They'll know how irresponsible I am

Michelle's Notes

8:33 PM
God, I feel sad at the thought of a day with just my thoughts, and I don't know when that's going to go away.

11:00 AM
Today I turned 25 and it kind of freaks me out.
Also, I put on my pants backwards.

So far, 25 is hard.

< Michelle's Notes

9:11 PM
The 25 Year Old List
(as written by my friends):

Rent a convertible
Learn a new skill
Become fluent in French
Become an aunt
Road trip
Buy a plane ticket the day of
Get engaged
Tattoo
New York
Host a dinner party
Hard reset
Steal something from a restaurant
Letterpress class
Pottery

4:59 PM
Fruit
Veggies
Veggie dip
Yogurt for fruit
Granola
Cheese and crackers
Stuff for quiche
Mimosas

< Michelle's Notes

11:33 PM
25 is texting my sister, crying in the car
while Rihanna's "Live Your Life" plays on the radio.

9:14 PM
I think the semester and work and all of the events were such a distraction, and now I've settled down, and I just feel it.

> Write a poem or essay about the heartbreak that lingers: when the body goes into shock and the adrenaline kicks in to keep you from feeling the full extent of your injuries.

Michelle's Notes

11:55 PM
I thought drinking made me sad, but tonight I didn't have a drop.

I want to be one of those people who can look back at the good times and be like, "yeah, cool." But I'm not. I want my memories pulled from my head in silvery strings. And I don't want to keep them safe. I want them gone.

The pain resides not only in what was, but in what was imagined. What was planned. It seems now like they were plans not only never realized, but never even possibilities.

I understand a broken arm. And I understand a cut thigh. I understand a broken friendship. But these matters go much deeper than all of it. These matters cut deep to who am and where I am. And not knowing even the next step.

I've begun making lists for myself because it helps with the tough days. I will go to sleep now and God, I beg you to have mercy on my dreams. And then tomorrow I will get up and run a race I shouldn't run, and I'll smile like it's some big deal.

Lord, I'm tired of lists, and I'm tired of failing more miserably every day. I just want a quiet heart. I need a heart of peace.

< Michelle's Notes

6:25 PM
Sparkling
Pregnancy
Decaf

10:17 PM
Maybe if I write you mini-love letters or poems,
it won't seem so bizarre and sad to me.

I don't know you yet, but I long for the day when you're beside me, and I'm too busy smiling and touching your cheek to fall asleep yet.

Wherever you are in this moment, I hope you feel my love.

< Michelle's Notes

8:14 AM
Bell pepper
Onions
Garlic

3:29 a.m.
I was at the Barnes & Noble, and I used the bathroom where you have to stand up real quick when you're done peeing because instead of a stall, it's just a glass room. The directions say pull your pants up quickly! but I struggle to get my jeans over my butt some days, so I was slow. When I turned around, there was this creep smirking at me on the other side of the wall.

I reported him, but they couldn't catch up with him. Then me and a bunch of people slept in the Barnes & Noble in sleeping bags as if it were a normal occurrence, and three guys tried to attack the place over night.

They didn't realize I was still awake.

I alerted our group, and we seized them. One of the guys turned out to be super hot, and I was like, "Hot Guy, why would you do that?" And then I recognized him as the smirking creep!

He laughed and said it was him the whole time and that he would have gotten away with it if I hadn't been awake. I said, "What? This isn't Scooby Doo, you idiot!"

But I can't remember what he said after that.

Then I house-sat for a cat that sang.

◁ Michelle's Notes

11:25 PM
upstairs neighbor jumping

12:28 PM

When I was in eighth grade, I passed out and fell face-first into the pew in front of me, my forehead bouncing back off the wood. Apparently, the sound echoed throughout the church, but mass didn't stop. It can't stop; it's a rule in the cannon or something. I woke up to a stranger taking my pulse, insisting I eat a peppermint covered in lint from the bottom of her purse.

Church meant getting sick. It meant suffocating and time stopping. "Claustrophobia" they'd called it. I didn't know what that word meant; I just knew that I hated Sunday mornings. I confessed this to my sister once and she told me that if I hated church, I hated Jesus.

It was convicting. And very Catholic.

What she couldn't know, what none of us could know, was there was more than just claustrophobia going on. Still, I accepted her assessment and took it on as my own. I would learn to love church because, I did, in fact, love Jesus. He died for me. I'd been taught that, although I didn't really understand why or what it meant.

For years I knew how to handle it. I knew not to lock my knees and to eat something more substantial than sugar cubes, but my stomach still twisted. I still felt sick. The cathedral's high ceilings couldn't stop the room from closing in on me.

Church overwhelmed me. I looked for quick fixes and tricks to stay upright in front of God and keep my gaze on the cross, but even the idea of going made me nervous.

So I stopped going altogether.

Until I moved to Baltimore, I thought this was my whole story. This was my relationship with God—complicated by sugar and taste aversions to a tradition that instilled a passion for guilt within me.

6:40 PM
Siri, how can you help me organize things?

< Michelle's Notes

11:33 PM
Scott at Anchors Down
Big Bertha stuck in Seattle
Minivan
Sam

7:30 AM

15 push ups

30 bicep curls (8 lbs.)

Triceps behind the head lifts
30 at 8 lbs.

15 shoulder lifts
5 lbs.

Back shrugs
30 at 8 lbs.

30 band squeezes
Blue band

20 supermans

128 lbs.

< **Michelle's Notes**

9:58 PM

God, why did you bring me here? I do not know how to do this on my own. I constantly think of wanting children. Of a future. Possibilities of things that don't exist. That cannot, will not, exist.

And each day it lingers, I hold my breath. My focus is taken from you and what you *are* doing in my life. I'm belittling all you've given me.

But Lord, the struggle is real. It's a constant back and forth. And I'm tired of fighting it.

Please Lord, lead me not into temptation.

12:45 AM
The city in the city

⟨ Michelle's Notes

6:04 AM
God, why would you do this to me? Why did you bring me to Baltimore and put me in a place that is so damn hard to be in. Why is he *so everywhere?* Why is me being included actually making me feel so left out?

I hate this.

I feel like I'm tackling it all on my own. Where are you in this confusion and pain? Why would I keep going to church when it hurts to go there?

I feel like I've done my part of it.

3:35 AM
Dropbox
Brick Bodies
Hulu
Verizon
BGE
Bare Minerals
Nature's snacks
Rent
Ford
Insurance
Groceries
Restaurants
Haircuts
Paypal
Victoria's Secret
Match.com
Nordstrom
Barnes & Noble

< Michelle's Notes

12:38 AM
I may have a mouse in my house. Can that happen in a second floor apartment?

I'm really hoping someone lives under my bed at this point.

9:25 AM
I have a mouse in my house

< Michelle's Notes

3:33 PM
Go to grocery list
Cleaning schedule
Total declutter
Know French
Write notes regularly

9:35 AM
Amanda's cat is coming over for a play date with the mouse tonight.

< Michelle's Notes

7:22 PM
Masking tape
Toothpaste

5:03 AM

I just woke up with a mouse on me, but I'm okay.

No, I'm not okay! It was ON ME.

I was sleeping on my back on the couch because the bedroom didn't feel safe. I woke up to the pitter patter of feet across the sheet and freaked out and started screaming immediately. In my effort to swipe him off of me, I tangled us both up in the sheet, binding my arms. I threw myself off the couch, trying to crawl my way out. I don't know what happened to the mouse at that point.

I screamed for at least three minutes straight like someone was attacking me. It concerns me slightly that none of my neighbors knocked on the door or called the cops.

< Michelle's Notes

4:08 PM
Running shoes

11:25 AM
I saw him again. He ran out of my closet. I've cleaned more and put steel wool in the hole. I also got peppermint oil, which is supposed to hurt their little noses, and I plugged in those sonar repellent devices in most of the outlets. (They say you only need one per room, but I don't trust it.)

No signs of him this morning.

< Michelle's Notes

8:38 PM

I have been cleaning around the clock. If I can get everything spotless, I don't think the mouse will want to stay here anymore. He will simply take his little mouse-sized suitcase and move on out. Here's what I'm struggling with though: is it better for me to see him move out (say in a trap) or for me just to never see him again and assume he's found new digs (but always wonder if he's still here)?

I don't like hearing him at night, so I've been sleeping with Pandora on to cover any sounds of his little feet or nibbles or jeering. Also, I've kept the lights on in my bedroom (dimmed, but with every corner illuminated just in case). This is helpful, except now that I can't hear him, I'm afraid that I'm going to wake up and he'll be snuggled up to me, his little mouse body cradling the opposite side of the body pillow. But I can't lie there in dark silence half-asleep, waiting for his pitter-patter either.

It always comes back to this: is it better to know or to not know?

> I am not one for confrontation. I do not like speaking about hard things or the lump that forms in my throat when tears find my eyes. I don't like the way that men's faces change when my eyes tear,

effectively steering the conversation to something less than honest if only to stop the crying. I wonder if the mouse is a guy mouse or a girl mouse.

The power just went out. How is this my life? Now what? I'm in the dark with a mouse who may be agitated by the smell of peppermint.

―――

I've filled the apartment with candlelight—it's actually quite nice—but what if the mouse runs across one and knocks it down and starts a fire? That's totally something he would do.

―――

I'm using my battery-dying phone to play music just to let the mouse know I'm still awake even though the lights are off, but now I feel uncomfortable because there's candlelight and I'm playing music and this is starting to feel like a weird romantic evening with the mouse. But maybe he's uncomfortable, too, and he'll just leave.

< Michelle's Notes

2:59 AM
How do I write anything else when my heart is focused on one thing?

God, I feel like a petulant little child, continuing to be mad at you until I get my way. And God, I've asked you in many different ways to take this away. I don't have the words to form this right, and I'm so angry with you that it's hard for me to talk it through, but just take it.

Turn my heart. Take it away. Give me peace.

Please just show up in a powerful way.

11:23AM
I'm so ready just to relax and party and not have a mouse in my house.

⟨ **Michelle's Notes**

2:10 PM
Bring nails to work

10:53 AM

Grandma is dead, and everyone is asking really strange questions:

Why are you going to the funeral?

> Is that strange? It can't be.
> That cannot be a weird thing; otherwise, we wouldn't plan funerals.

Were you close?

> Were we close? Well, when I called her (which wasn't enough), and I said, "Hello, Grandma, it's Michelle." I didn't have to add, "Michelle Junot."

Your dad's mom or your mom's mom?
How old was she?
What did she die from?
Are you okay?

And they're all sorry. Everyone's always sorry. Real sorry. I've never met someone who was glad another person died. Sure, there's talk of "ending suffering" and "better places" and even when you believe that—and I do—you aren't glad. "Glad" isn't the right emotion.

⟨ Michelle's Notes

What if I answered with lies? Is that a normal thing to wonder? To think about? Like what if I lied about the circumstances of my grandmother's death, made it more tragic than a 93 year old dying of relatively natural causes?

And is it fair to mourn her when I couldn't be bothered to see her when she was alive? Because that's the question really: Were we close?

That's the real question sandwiched in between all the others. That's the one that I ask over and over. The one that keeps me awake. It's the kind of question that determines the kind of person you are, at least to yourself.

My grandmother is dead and I'm mourning her. I miss her. I cried when it was the end, and I realized there wasn't any more time.

There wasn't time to get on a plane. There wasn't time to ask her what she meant in the last line of the letter she wrote me that I hadn't even read at that point.

> (I'd cashed the enclosed check, but put the letter on the table beside my bed to read "at the right time." I hadn't written a thank you note yet; I hadn't called her. It was on my to-do list. I wanted to read the letter first and then reference something she

said in the letter. Now I know that if I had read it, I would have asked her about the last line.)

What does the last line mean?
Why would she say that?

Someone asked me if she planned her own funeral. I shook my head, disgusted. *Who does that? Morbid much?* "It's so much easier when they do that," she replied.

Apparently, little did I know, Grandma *had* actually planned her own funeral. She bought a very inexpensive, unadorned coffin from some monks in Pennsylvania.

Had I known, I could have picked it up and just brought it with me on the plane from Baltimore. That's terrible and weird! I scold myself in my mother's voice.

Why do you think things like that at times like this?

At a time like what, though? Grandma is dead and we're concerned with things like caskets and cleaning out her house after the funeral, securing the jewelry from her jewelry box to remember her.

She left me the metal from her neck. Literally. Before

< Michelle's Notes

they closed the casket, they took the metal off her neck and handed it to me, and I put it on mine. Heavy, I thought. *This is heavy.* "The chain is fragile," they said. "She didn't have it on a proper chain—really needs a rope chain. But it's valued at over $300!"

    Why are they telling me this?

I wanted to make a joke about pawning it, but I didn't. They wouldn't know I was joking because they don't actually know me. They're concerned with her money and her stuff (that I guess is now their stuff), and I'm just missing Grandma.

    It's unfair to assume they aren't. I know they are. I know this is just a disgusting coping mechanism. But still, it hurts.

I want to be like one of those families that sit around with coffee—because I always want coffee—sharing our favorite memories.

On the way back to Lafayette, with my immediate clan in the car—my peeps, if you will (they won't)—I tried to make us this family. I asked everyone to share a happy memory of my grandmother.

    My brother remembered her playing toys with him;
        my mom said she pictured Grandma waving from her rocker on the porch;
            and I talked about the joy of staying up late with Grandma, watching all the shows on cable we didn't catch.

My dad shared two very early childhood memories—
one of his mother and another of his father. In a world
where I've heard every Junot story at least seven
times, these surprised me. I'd never heard him talk
about his family this way.

> They were delicate and gentle: memories of first
> knowing love.

>> Something changed in me then. My heart felt
>> different than it has before, and I saw my dad
>> in a way I never want to forget.

We rarely get to the nitty gritty in my family. We rarely deal
with emotions. I think the first time my parents really knew
about my fear and anxiety was when I published a book
about hard things and sent it to them two days before I
sent it to the printer. I didn't sleep, wondering what they
would say, both grateful and regretful of our distance.

My heart longs in all kinds of directions. But never
actually where I think it leans. God romances me with
surprises and turns and unexpected twists.

> It's like the timing of all this: the joy of my precious
> nephew joining the world paired with the loss of
> my grandmother. It's almost too much, too perfect.

< Michelle's Notes

The moment of realization is what hurts most. Putting her in the ground, and having to walk away. That's the kind of moment I don't know how we get through without the Holy Spirit pulling and guiding us.

>And then such anger!

A family feud as soon as the last flower was dropped in the tomb. Why couldn't we all just spend the rest of the day together? That is in my blood. That's where I come from, but luckily, by the grace of God, that's not who I am.

>And that's also why I grieve, because life is not how my grandmother wanted it.

She left a broken world that she so desperately wanted to control, and I have that same fighting, fierce, passive aggressive spirit buried in my bones. I don't quite know what to do with that except to constantly push it back down.

My grandmother wrote me a letter, and I read it on the morning of her funeral. It gave me closure that she loved me. That she was proud of me, and that she understood me in a way I could never articulate when we talked. It told me we were connected in all the ways I feared we were not.

It told me she knew where I stood and she was proud. But, of course, it also hurt something fierce.

Closure aches. Don't let anyone tell you any different. Closure is helpful in that it forces your feet forward and now you're facing the right way, but damn it stings. Closure is running or walking or crawling away from something that mattered. Something that defined you. Something that held you to that part of the earth in the first place.

I think about my plans to call her this summer to track our family history. I think about all the stories of hers I wanted to write down. Are they still the truth if I write them down now, only from my memory of her telling me? Were they ever really truth? She was the last one of her family, or the last one that counts, at least to me.

I think about calling her now, but I know she won't answer. The thought surprises me though. Why did I just think about that? She's dead. I've already said she's dead, right?

My grandmother is dead, and I keep asking really strange questions.

⟨ Michelle's Notes

7:50 AM
The way water spills more heavily to one side than the other
How can so much happen between two Sundays
It's strange that we should plant flowers purposefully
The idea of robots and missing something
We are missing something big
The quest for Atlantis
Age-old idea of taking things for granted. And yet it hits hard, with a force.
It rolls over like waves, with renewed gusto

12:05 AM
My grandmother lived 14 years without my grandfather. I wonder if she had lonely nights the same way I have and why I didn't call her to talk about those things. She would have welcomed the conversation, I think.

I consider the nights I couldn't sleep, worrying about marrying or not marrying a man 12 years my senior and the fear of falling in love with someone only to lose them, and yet, here was my grandmother with this whole other life after her husband. She had a life full of weddings and deaths, births of eight great-grandchildren, and she saw me become the woman I am—from afar, but a woman no less.

My grandmother taught me the importance of things like phones and Mardi Gras and taxes, but more than that, she taught me pride and love and endurance. She taught me faith. She taught me to be fearless, she taught me strength, and she was insistent that I always date everything. She showed me that life didn't end with the death of my grandfather, though I know she missed him in ways I cannot even begin to understand.

At her brother's funeral, I stood on the other side of the mausoleum while the rifle shots were fired in three slow rounds, the metal bouncing on the marble floor around me. Her body rock with sobs. How many people had she buried now?

My cousin turned to me and said, "She's thinking about Pa Jack." We couldn't comfort her; we could only watch as the old men gathered their shell casings and the flag was folded into small, neat triangles. Another one for the shelf.

Grandma taught me grief and my grief grows for her now.

There was comfort that came from knowing she was always just a phone call away—even if I couldn't be bothered to make the call. There was comfort in knowing her house was always the same—our toys just where we left them should we ever want to leave this life, retreat from adulthood, and spend a week at Grandma's. That's gone now, buried beneath the earth with my grandfather and another cousin I never knew.

She is gone. Grandma is dead. And I simply don't know how to live in a world without her.

3:50 AM
Cut the feels pieces

5:45 PM

Waiting is active. Waiting is a whole body activity. Waiting is preparing. Getting ready. Ready to move. To sprint. Waiting is a bending at the knees. A bowing in worship. Waiting is today. Today is waiting and being ready because I have no idea what tomorrow will bring.

Tomorrow could be moving. Tomorrow could be running away or toward, but running all the same. And I wonder,

>   Will I be ready?

12:53 PM

A plane fell out of the sky and still the world went on. A day later, my hometown was on lockdown for a bomb threat and a suspicious device in the park where I learned to run. The same small town that only just mourned the kidnapping and death of a pretty blond girl who was just riding her bike.

And a plane fell out of the sky!

When there's a school shooting—and there always is—I turn off the news. I don't want to hear about it anymore. I don't want to picture the children I don't have or my nephew's face. I don't want to empathize with the parents who live those nightmares because the small glimpse I have from their tear-stained faces is enough to crush me completely.

We are all numb. And more and more, we are strangers in a way that we cannot come back from.

And a plane. There was a plane that fell from the sky and another one that just disappeared. It disappeared with questions and loved ones, and we buried those people with conspiracy theories and opinions and Facebook statuses that ultimately did nothing for anyone.

< **Michelle's Notes**

When I look at the photos, it's not the wreckage that ruins me. When I look at those pictures, I see an abstract installation at an over-priced museum. I can't make those images link back to my many trips seated on the blue Delta fabric, with strangers and children behind me. The wreckage does not move me; it's the people left behind that cripples.

It's the woman who's covering her face with her hands. This is her life. She's a real person and this is her life right now. And watching her grief on the TV in my apartment, alone, on the other side of the world, makes me lonely. Maybe the answer is not to shut her out, not really, but let her and her story take hold of my heart beyond my morning cup of coffee.

In a world without faith I find myself apologizing for it or tiptoeing around it, confessing silently to God that I do not know how to do better.

There's another image of busses carrying relatives of the dead to and from wherever they're going. A holding area? Do they speak to one another? Do they start crying all over again, but this time together? I'm inconsolable when I cry. When I really cry. Is anyone able to console them?

I remember the sharp-dressed funeral director closing the casket at my grandmother's funeral. I'd thought this part came at the end of mass. I thought there was more time—another hour to work through a lifetime of questions. I couldn't catch my breath, surprised by my sudden grief and unwillingness to live in a world without her voice.

There's another picture of all the luggage from the plane. Ordinary luggage piled on top of one another with no one to retrieve it. It reminds me of the shoes piled in a room at the Holocaust museum. It's all very ghostly, haunting. We work our whole lives for things that we cannot take with us when we go.

I'm staring again at the photo-woman covering her face with her hands, wishing I could hug her and tell her she doesn't have to hide her hurt.

< Michelle's Notes

9:39 PM
Twin Peaks and runaway truck ramps

6:32 AM
iPhone for running
Headphones and all that jazz
Workout book
Tote for the beach
Strings for bikini

< Michelle's Notes

8:15 AM
I don't care what you call me by David Ford.

9:06 AM
There's a mouse in my bag.
I'm going to be late.

< Michelle's Notes

10:09 AM
Bag in dumpster, mouse MIA.

2:19 PM
Chicken or turkey

Michelle's Notes

3:13 AM
A mouse trumps almost any other problem.

Any and all thoughts or prayers I have about my writing or relationships or lack thereof: gone.

I am only worried about a mouse tracking me, finding me, transforming into some kind of amazon anaconda and eating me. One ran across my person once, so that's pretty much the same thing.

Everyone keeps saying: he can't hurt you. The mouse can't hurt you. Ever have a mouse on you? No? You lose your right to an opinion on the situation then.

Everything starts to look like mice: clips on the floor, bookmaking tools. Even impossible things: ink pens, my own feet.

You challenge everything in your apartment: wait...whose remote is that? I don't remember that remote, who put that remote here?

I also start blaming him for all my problems: he's the reason my Internet has been so terrible lately. The reason I can't keep a man. That jerk took my phone charger!

Heard a car swerve right outside my window: mouse.

He's ruined bags for me.

He's taught me how I deal with fear: I let it consume me. I let the what-ifs rule who I am. I err on the side of seizing a false sense of control over my life

‹ Michelle's Notes

11:39 AM
Wind
Trees
Colors swirling
Not letting up
Fleeting before my eyes

10:01 PM
Deciding to sleep in the middle of the bed.

‹ Michelle's Notes

11:09 PM
I can hear my neighbor through the wall in a loud, one-sided conversation. Must be a video chat—her voice is raised, but not in anger as if she were screaming into the phone. I can only catch pieces of the conversation—lawyers…if you keep crying like this, I'll have to go—and then, "Happy birthday!" in a sing-song way. In a genuine, my-face-is-smiling way. It's the way you'd say it to a child.

It's 11 PM. A child's birthday would have to be on the West Coast for that to make sense.

And then, sadder, "Yeah. I'm still here."

> I reach into my bedside drawer and pull out earplugs. This seems too private—even after quiet hours. I have my own loneliness to deal with; I can't add the homesickness of my neighbor through a wall. I'll smile in the morning when we cross paths and try not to think about the video chat (and try even harder not to think about how thin these walls are or all the times she must have clearly heard voices from this side).

2:10 PM
Hat
Scarves
Gloves
Running thing
Tampons
Fruit
Advil

< Michelle's Notes

4:20 AM
Traveling is bloodshot eyes in the morning and promising never to do this again.

7:03 AM
15.4%
124.5 lbs.
21.4 BMI

Thigh 22.5
Calf 13.5
Ankle 8
Butt 36.5
Waist 28
Hips 34.5
Bicep 10
Forearm 9.5
Shoulder 15
Neck 13.5

Michelle's Notes

7:45 PM

Sorting through text messages and photos of smiling faces of three different men I've had feelings for—two more than all the others—is difficult at best. It's a lump I swallow down, filed into the proper folder to be stored away until that chapter is ready to be written from some perspective other than hurt.

It's not far off; it's close. I can see that because I have a certain amount of joy looking at the pictures. But it isn't here yet. And so, I have to wait.

File the pictures. Swallow down the lump. Remember that I am loved, even if not by them.

I look at my beautiful baby nephew, sitting next to me, who has only just discovered he has hands. I know that my time is coming. Until then, I click save and close that box.

4:00 PM
Omission

< Michelle's Notes

8:15 AM
My body/exercise
Work
Money
The apartment
To-do lists
Feeling overwhelmed and kind of lost
Going through the motions
Very little energy
A lot of anger
Feeling like I'm constantly failing
Not living up to my own or my perception of his standards
Judging myself through a single person's eyes
Really lonesome
Jealous

1:04 PM
Some songs fill me with a deep nostalgia and loneliness no matter where I am or who I am with. "Time Marches On" will always be one of those songs.

It takes me back to the early nineties, to a clean, but quiet house on Saturday afternoons when I was somewhere, doing something quietly with the cat by my side. Mom's in her sewing room, and I don't know where anyone else is.

It occurs to me that I always know exactly where my mother was or wasn't in my memories, but I don't know where any of the others were.

< Michelle's Notes

12:33 PM
Part of me enjoys telling stories, but I wonder if they can ever really be "true" or if I'm simply creating a definitive version to tell over and over again more easily.

8:35 PM
Job 38

< Michelle's Notes

10:39 PM
Deleted old phone contacts
Tomorrow: delete old Facebook friends

8:34 AM
Email link to chick

< Michelle's Notes

1:59 AM
MVA in the woods
Get back at night
Woman stops you to use your phone
Think it's a trap
Run back
Get there as they're closing
Return something, get money, share it with the boy
Become then sort of an orphan
Dancing on a trampoline
Doing spins
Finally get it
Communicate the perfect piece
The whipping of the spin becomes too much
and you're flying into glass and all around

Come back bionic
They've redeveloped end and your entire body

You'll still be a ballerina with bent back lumps

8:40 PM
MOVIES I HAVEN'T SEEN:

Indiana Jones

< Michelle's Notes

12:28 PM
Stuff to talk to Joshua about:
timeline; I'm confused.

9:06 AM
Another mouse ate his way through the insulation to get in.

I'm beginning to think it's the same mouse and he has a map to my apartment.

⟨ Michelle's Notes

8:10 PM
My nephew loves music.
He loves bad music.
He loves music that comes from my sister's lovely, but out-of-tune mouth.
He loves French music that I sing to him even though I got a D in my college Français class.

He loves when we hum if he's crying.
He loves Pandora.
He loves the songs even when we change the words as long as we keep a steady beat.

It calms him.
It makes him smile.
It lets him know that we're still here, with him, that we hear him.

Singing to him, watching him change from crying—for any number of reasons—to a quiet whimper, to a smile, to a full out giggle sometimes as he locks your eyes and you sing to him, it brings tears to the backs of my eyes.

It moves something in the core of me that I can't quite explain, and I don't think it's just because his blood and my blood share similar properties.

His mother, my sister, has explained to me that while all crying babies upset her, there's something desperate about her own child's cry. There's something that will make her move mountains to figure out how to stop his crying.

When he cries, my heart doesn't break on that same line. Mostly, noise upsets me, except, funnily enough, music. Blaring music is the only thing that pushes down the lump in my throat sometimes.

There's a movement to it.

There's an involuntary heart rhythm that it creates when I feel stuck in an emotion or painful experience. Whether I like it or not, something has to stir within me if I'm moving to music.

I wonder if the same thing is happening to my nephew, if we share that bond somehow.

He will not have memories of our last 10 days together, so I'm trying to remember everything for the both of us.

❮ Michelle's Notes

2:17 PM
The best stories seek truth at their heart

8:15 PM
freelance: done & caught up
new schedule and goals for new year
wanted to figure out therapy stuff
figure out joshua stuff
wanted to get off facebook and insta and all that
wanted to have all my files cleaned up
be healthy
get wyatt's pictures
have a to-do list for saturday
decluttering
rest and restore
write & finish those pieces
get caught up with writers & words
make a master to-do list
not worry about work
finish translating 25
pray
spend time with wyatt
be independent still

⟨ Michelle's Notes

5:43 AM
Cornered a mouse

10:15 AM
Caught the mouse! Dropping him off in the woods and going to work.

< Michelle's Notes

8:04 AM
Write freelance articles
Clean up
Laundry
Books picked up
Why didn't I sleep well?
Alarm in bed with me
Didn't get up when should have
Not enough water
DISCIPLINE

7:26 AM
Sheets
Body wash
Coffee

< Michelle's Notes

4:47 PM
Paint trim or walls first?

4:27 AM
Single-leg glute bridge
Cable row

Reverse lunge step up
DB shoulder press

Reverse hyper extension
Lying leg raise
Oblique twist
Ball crunches

< Michelle's Notes

6:50 AM
Wash clothes
Finish making chicken salad and food
Charge all devices

2:39 PM
Roll up your sleeves

Michelle's Notes

9:34 PM
What do I know?
What are the facts?
What is true?
What leaps am I making?
Am I being selfish because I didn't get what I want?

If I had done this, what would I expect of someone who is loving, kind, and gentle?

Have I prayed about it?
Have I really prayed about it?
Am I worrying and creating problems where they don't exist?
If God is in control, what could I possibly be upset about?
Am I letting unfair expectations fuel my emotions and letting emotions run me?

> Hey Michelle,
> why don't you just chill,
> take a breath,
> count to 10, and
> pray for someone besides yourself?

4:52 AM
Sleepy
Cold
Overwhelmed
Already late

< Michelle's Notes

6:05 AM
Being sluggish and tired
Worrying
Using my phone
Starting projects but not finishing them
On email/text messages
Not dealing with things right when they happen
Having conversations before they happen
Not going directly to the source when I'm worried

8:59 AM
I like to think I put my trust in God
but really, I'm functionally trusting myself
and then I screw up
and I'm all shocked by it
because I have this unrealistic view of my own heart

< Michelle's Notes

7:13 PM
So introverted

6:08 AM
Gym
Coffee plus smoothie
Drop stuff off at house
Target
Dry cleaning
Whole Foods
House for cleaning & work

< Michelle's Notes

9:22 PM
Scared off like when an animal approaches you to sniff you and you move your hand or body too soon or quickly or in some unexpected manner
and the animal runs away and you have to say,

"No! No, it's okay. Come here; I'm not going to hurt you."

It either trusts you then, walking slowly back, or it waits to watch what you'll do next.
But it has to be on its own terms.

That's how it is with me.

6:47 AM
Clean up
Make grocery list
Exercise
Read and write a little
Make to-do lists for the week

5:00 PM
Lying to myself
What he said about prayer
Argumentative—exception, not the rule
Being a child
Pattern
Missing the point when I say "don't give up on me"
Foundational
Can't move forward

Abide

9:17 PM
Write about the heart
   and longing
      and the way we depict this,
         the physicality of something we cannot touch
         but we call it the heart.

And the brain,
   how they are at war with one another sometimes
   but we need both to live.

We need both, and we shouldn't settle for them being at war.

We should long to give them both up—easier said than done—so they might have a chance at working powerfully together for a glory higher than our own.

< Michelle's Notes

8:22 PM
Heart is linked to emotions. Head is linked to behavior.

If we want heart-level change—and I do—but also don't want to react based on "feelings," then how do we actually get there? I guess we choose to believe when we don't feel it—using our heads to affect our hearts.

I think real change goes deeper and is more complicated than I first thought. It feels like there is no simple understanding of "being a Christian" and it's mega frustrating when people make it seem so.

> Surrender, give up control, believe, repent, repeat—it feels like my heart and brain are daily ripped from my body, renewed, and then Scotch-taped back together. I feel like an imposter most days. I don't feel shiny and new. I feel sinful or angry or bitter.

But I will keep getting up and trying again and trying not to "try again," but "believe more."

Reminds me of getting to the middle of Thesis and thinking

> *Everyone must be lying.*

There's no way we're going to finish a book in a semester.
This can't be true.

But it was true.

Maybe this is kind of like that, but on a cosmic scale of salvation.

< Michelle's Notes

5:58 PM
Tampons—
    cheapest I've found are 16 cents a piece (with coupons)

Do not buy until August
    Cat litter

Stocked up, do not buy until Christmas:
    Tampons
    Bobby pins
    Hair ties
    Laundry detergent

Being a woman is expensive.

9:08 PM
He doesn't think I'm genuine.
God, that's hard.

Michelle's Notes

8:57 AM
Is a willingness to suffer a marker of love? I mean true suffering, not just everyday "this is hard" stuff. Not suffering from foolishness.

> Why aren't we suffering more if it's a true marker?
> Why do we turn away when it gets hard?
> What is real faith?

It's like *The Walking Dead*. They're worried about "getting weak," or of forgetting what it's like outside the gates.

9:54 PM
We come at everything from different sides of the coin —
or at least a lot of the stuff that matters.

> BUT THAT'S AMAZING!

Because otherwise we would be so blind to certain aspects of ourselves
and never get to go deeper in love with Christ
or learn to love one another.

> We would get along in a surface way, but never really figure this out.

7:53 AM
To say
    I know that already
        is really to say
            stop talking to me.

                What you have to say adds nothing to me so I don't want to be bothered by it.
                I don't care what it means to you, or why you feel the need to share.

I only want to listen in as much as I can get something out of it.

3:23 PM
God, I trust you. But it hurts.

Michelle's Notes

8:50 PM
Eating the food that makes me sick—breaking out in rashes

>Orlando—
>
>Can everyone just shut up for a minute?
>Moments of silence.
>We don't know everything. We don't know how to fix it.

The medicine they prescribed for me has a side effect: itchy rashes. It's a Band-Aid that won't hold.

>What's the real problem?

I don't have answers. I have faith, and honestly, I have a lot more questions. And I plead with God in my prayers to help me understand this un-understandable thing. But just take a minute,

>to shut up.

Just shut up. Stay still. Stop talking and listen.

Listen to the world sobbing and crying out and trying to prove its point. We don't know how to fix this, but I dare say the first step is looking to yourself—not at how great and wonderful you are, not how much you are worth, but how you harbor hate in your heart.

How you long to be right.

What you believe and how that affects the others around you.

I believe in a Savior and it's a good thing, because damn if I don't completely screw up by 7 a.m. with hate in my heart and self-righteousness that goes so deep that it surprises me.

It's startling. I'm not a good person, but I think none of us are. We can't do this alone. We can't fix this with a Facebook status.

So shut up. Do a little self-discovery without updating your status, and let's do the hard work of loving others—especially those who completely disagree with us.

Because listen, the world isn't about you, and it's not about me. We live at the center of our universes and then we're shocked by isolation and hate.

But really? Is it really that shocking?

< Michelle's Notes

2:47 AM
"Wait patiently for the Lord.
Be brave and courageous.
Yes, wait patiently for the Lord."

Psalms 27:14

7:13 AM
Gettysburg
Niagara Falls
Acadia National Park
Mount Vernon
Shenandoah Caverns
Assateague Island

< Michelle's Notes

5:30 AM
Woke up from a bad dream immediately frustrated to be awake.

At least in the dream world, people know they're screwed up and they don't try to hide it.
In the real world, everyone's pretending they're not.

11:36 AM
Heavy whipping cream

⟨ Michelle's Notes

12:13 AM
For me, dreaming has become a platform to experience impossible realities over and over, replaying the outcomes with different variables.

> The outcome never changes from real life
> The dead ones are still dead
> The mistakes are still mistakes
> But the "we" there is always a little different

I was just in a dream, replaying something from my early childhood—something I'm not even sure ever happened—a restaurant scene with my mother right before I was born.

I was there in theory I guess and so I was able to be there in-dream but the chronology kept skipping like it does in dreams and now I wasn't watching my pregnant mother but a pregnant me at the table, talking about how I feel.

And my body in the dream knows the outcome—or the impossibility of it. My body has never known pregnancy and so the dream isn't going to end right. I know this—in the dream—so I start to look around.

Because this is my other trick. I look for the unfamiliar parts—or the slightly off parts. I let the people around me keep talking—I only have a moment before they stop and notice me not playing along. And that's when I felt it. I could feel his eyes on me—one of these things isn't like the other; one of these things doesn't belong. I saw him, hiding behind his menu. I smirked, now in on the secret, and walked right up to him.

The grandfather I did not get the chance to know. (I've now known him more in my dreams than I ever did in life.) This silly peekaboo game. The one from when I was three. The only real—although maybe not real—memory I have of him paired with me as a grown woman.

"I saw you there," I say. I hug him and he smirks. I found him. This is our game. Time is speeding up—only another moment before the dream catches up or memory or brain waves figure out that I know that my brain knows that I'm dreaming and it's time to wake up. "Smile for a picture," someone says. "It's your birthday!"

And in the moment, I smiled and reached down to my nonexistent belly—my first memories and future hopes and subsequent fears all coming in at the same moment—and I know that no picture of this moment actually exists and can't exist and it's all about to fall apart.

< Michelle's Notes

"No!" I shout, turning back to him and reaching out to shield us from the photo ending. The camera flashes and I wake off my pillow gasping.

Waking up, I know I've had five of those back to back — there was one about being upside down in the snow, trying to find my way to the surface before I drowned, as if in water. One has a boyfriend that perpetually blends with a husband on that side of sleep, and one is just a hall of mirrors of scenes from my life that are the most traumatic that play over and over and over, shaping me daily in this pointless kind of movie loop with different choices but exactly the same outcome.
It's annoying really, as if to say, "You know why you are this way, right?"

Of course I know.
That's why I don't like to go to sleep.

10:33 AM
Church bells ringing
and nothing is happening.

< Michelle's Notes

4:29 PM
If we didn't have trials, then we might be tempted to think we don't need God or that we are god, so I'm grateful for God's sovereignty and grace in that. It's just hard. I get stuck and don't know how to process my fear and lack of trust.

8:00 PM

So this class I'm taking is humbling. For years I've wanted a "better relationship" with other people, and I thought *they* were the reason I didn't have one. If they would only x, y, and z...

But I've been the roadblock. I have totally judged them and thought myself more "put together" than them when they have never once made me feel inferior.

< Michelle's Notes

10:55 PM
I spend my time
texting
checking social media
making lists
moving things around
organizing clutter
complaining
not using my words effectively
cleaning
worrying
talking
being vain
clearing out emails
spending money
being lazy
watching tv
making plans
overthinking
saving
trying to be my own god

1:44 AM
A bug in bed with me

< Michelle's Notes

9:29 PM
"This is my command—be strong and courageous!
Do not be afraid or discouraged.
For the Lord your God is with you wherever you go."

Joshua 1:9

9:57 AM
Reading through my old journals is awkward.

The pain from that version of myself is so palpable, it brings a lump to my throat. I remember that girl tossing and turning and begging for sleep. And in a lot of ways, I'm that same girl tumbling, tumbling, tumbling over herself, but there's a joy in it that keeps me from worrying about the eventual fall.

There's a calmness and a familiarity to the pain that keeps it from stealing my breath away. I lost all that I was sure of, but gained everything I didn't realize I was searching for.

I've always been looking for Him; I only called Him by a different name.

Acknowledgements

I'm indebted to many people—not only for their love and support throughout the course of this project, but also for their encouragement and friendship over the last five years of my life as Baltimore became my home.

First, thank you Lord. You not only "put up" with my ramblings, overthinking, mistrust, and attitude, but you also love me abundantly. Some days—most days—it's all I can do to remember and wrap my mind around the fact that you sent Christ for people like me who are so not put together, but I'll happily spend the rest of my life engaged in that process. In any case, thank you for being God and for reminding me often that I am not.

Thank you to all the people who kept me going throughout the project with their genuine interest and excitement over the collection. Without your *"Oh, I totally feel that way sometimes,"* or, *"Yes! Why is that so hard?"* or, *"I can't wait to read this."* I don't think I would have gotten to this point. (And I'm now glad I did.)

Special thanks goes to Hannah and Alissa for reading the manuscript in its most vulnerable state and sharing your feedback and affirmation even then.

And of course, thank you Mike, Ian, and Mason Jar Press. You guys were the first to believe in this project—even before I did—and you've supported me as editors and friends every step of the way. I owe you more than book sales. Ultimately, I'm just grateful you're my friends. Thanks for putting up with my missed deadlines, my not-so-sneaky addition of 100 pages of content to the "final draft," my attitude, and most-encouraging to me, for still liking me even after reading the notes we edited out.

Finally, thanks to you. Yes you. You with the book in your hand. You who have powered through to the very end (or who broke the rules and read this first). Without you, I'm just some girl with too much time on her hands and books in her basement. Thanks for making me a writer.

Also Available Through Mason Jar Press

Caligula's Playhouse by Stephen Zerance

Nihilist Kitsch by Mathew Falk

The Pop Culture Poems by Michael B. Tager

Visit us online at masonjarpress.xyz to learn more.